P9-BZH-963

D0002782

WILLIAMSBURG

CLB 848
© 1985 Illustrations and text: Colour Library Books Ltd.,
   Guildford, Surrey, England.
Text filmsetting by Acesetters Ltd., Richmond, Surrey, England.
Printed in Spain.
All rights reserved.
1985 edition published by Crescent Books, distributed by Crown Publishers, Inc.
ISBN 0 517 478145
h g f e d c b a
Dep.Leg.B-38.743-85

WILLIAMSBURG

Text by

Bill Harris

CRESCENT BOOKS
NEW YORK

Never ask an American where he is from. If he is from Virginia, he'll tell you without being asked. If he is not, why humiliate him?

Almost no one who was born in Virginia hasn't heard words to that effect. No one who has ever been to Virginia doesn't understand them. There is pride in every corner of the Old Dominion. But the corner where it is felt most strongly is between Norfolk and Fredericksburg, and it reaches its highest intensity in the peninsula formed by the York and James rivers. That is where America began. Why shouldn't they be proud?

There are dozens of historic sites in that triangle. The remnants of the first permanent English settlement in North America can still be seen at Jamestown. The battlefield where America finally won its independence from the Mother Country is nearby at Yorktown. The area is dotted with other battlefields important in the Civil War. The capital of the Confederacy is not far away at Richmond.

But in the center of it all is the historic monument more Americans recognize than any other, the second capital of the first colony, Williamsburg.

The amazing thing about Williamsburg is that no one thought of it sooner. Jamestown served as the colonial capital for nearly 100 years, and though it's a pretty place today, it was pretty awful back in the 17th century. It wasn't that it was a site casually selected. Three ships with about 140 immigrants aboard were blown into Chesapeake Bay by a storm on April 26, 1607. It took them until May 12 to find a likely place to land and establish their colony. They picked a peninsula on the James River because it was easy to defend against the Indians, who seemed hostile, and because deep water ran close enough to the shore to allow them to tie their boats to the trees on the shoreline. They probably should have moved on. The water wasn't fit to drink. The humidity was worse than oppressive. They had brought a few chickens along with them, but even they couldn't survive the living conditions. Mosquitoes could, though, and so could weevils who, in fact, thrived on the settlers' store of wheat. By the end of the summer, fifty of the original settlers were dead and the survivors were in the mood for killing each other.

Fortunately, they had some resourceful leaders, like Captain John Smith, and the Indians didn't prove to be as hostile as they had seemed at first. New colonists arrived and there was talk of moving further inland. But with new colonists came new reasons for conflict among them, and by the end of 1609 they had squabbled themselves into almost complete starvation. They managed to turn the Indians against them and by the following spring made a decision to abandon the colony and go home to England. By that point there were only sixty survivors.

They actually did leave on June 10, but before they were clear of the Bay, they met a little fleet of ships sent out from London with a new governor aboard, not to mention new settlers and new supplies.

The new governor, Lord Delaware, had strong ideas about law and order and by the end of the summer he had rebuilt Jamestown and given it a sense of style that affects some Virginians even today. The colony grew after that, and began to spread outward. Life wasn't without its problems. They had them with Indians and with each other. But they thrived in spite of their problems, and many families even grew wealthy. Within less than a dozen years they had their own representative form of government. It was called the General Assembly of Virginia. One of its two parts was a group of Councilors appointed by the London Company – the merchants in England who financed the settlement. The other, called the Burgesses, was composed of men elected by the freemen of the colony itself. The Governor, a royal appointee, had complete veto power, and no laws passed by the Assembly were considered valid without the approval of the London Company.

The Company was more interested in profits than a well-run colony. In the years between 1610 and 1622, 14,000 people went to Jamestown to find a new life. All but 1,000 of them found death. It was one of the great disasters in the history of mankind. No plague, no war has ever taken such a large proportion of a population in so short a time. The most terrible chapter in that story came in 1622 when the Indians went on the warpath and in a single night killed 350 men, women and children.

When the survivors asked the London Company for help, the response was to "send money, go to church, and quit complaining." The king finally responded by forcing the Company's investors to save the colony from starvation. They didn't move quickly enough to suit him and so he revoked their charter and took charge himself.

King James died a few months after that, to the relief of the Burgesses who knew of his opinion of representative government. His son, Charles I, was not much more enlightened about such things, but problems at home kept him distracted. In an almost absent-minded gesture, he told them that they could hold two annual elections. They did. Then they held a third and, when the king's wrath didn't come down on them, a fourth. After their tenth election, Charles took notice of them again. He decreed that no laws or taxes could be imposed without the approval of the General Assembly and reaffirmed that his appointed governor would, in turn, appoint the members of the Council. A point that eluded him was that the governor's appointees were by then all colonists. Unwittingly, Charles I established self-government in England's North American colonies.

Charles didn't seem to give a lot of thought to his selection of governors, but the colony survived. But not long before the king was tossed into prison by Oliver Cromwell, he made a fateful choice in the person of Sir William Berkeley. The governor was replaced twice during the Cromwell Protectorate, both times by men the Virginians violently disliked. The colonists were still loyal to the imprisoned king and when he was beheaded, the Assembly declared that his son, Charles II, was the new king, even though no such declaration was made back in London, and wouldn't be for nearly a dozen years.

During the years of the Protectorate, families still loyal to the monarchy were encouraged to find refuge in Virginia and a huge number answered the call. They all found a warm welcome from fellow Cavaliers, especially former governor Berkeley. When the monarchy was restored and Charles II was officially made king, Berkeley was reinstated as governor and the king had as loyal a group of subjects in Virginia as anywhere in his realm.

The Cavaliers were completely in charge. Anyone Berkeley liked could have the best plantations, the best-paying jobs in public service, even seats in the House of Burgesses. Under Berkeley's tenure, no elections were held for fifteen years.

It led to the first American Revolution. It all began exactly one hundred years before the second one.

It started with new Indian troubles. When the Senecas and Susquehannas began attacking outlying plantations, the governor turned a deaf ear to pleas for help. Forts that had been established were useless because money that had been appropriated to keep them in repair had found its way into Cavalier pockets instead.

The man who brought the planters together against the governor was a Cavalier himself, a former council member named Nathaniel Bacon. He formed his own militia and took care of the Indian problem, then he turned his attention to Jamestown. The governor had suspended him from the Council and branded him a traitor for taking the law into his own hands. Sensing that he had the support of most of the people, Bacon led a 250-man army into Jamestown demanding to see the governor. Berkeley finally agreed to pardon him, and gave him permission to keep on fighting Indians. But Bacon had no sooner left town with his men than the governor revoked the pardon and began saying nasty things about him again. Bacon was accurate in his perception that he had the support of the man in the street and by the time he got back to Jamestown with fire in his eye, he found the governor's mansion empty. Berkeley had fled to the Eastern Shore and Bacon seemed to have been left in charge.

When the Indian fighter left again, after having formed his own government, the governor came home with a small army. Bacon was able to drive him out again, and, as the governor's ships were sailing down the river, he burned Jamestown to the ground.

In a matter of weeks Bacon was dead of malaria, a common affliction in the mosquito-ridden Tidewater country. Berkeley was in charge again and began rounding up the rebels and hanging them. He hanged so many without the formality of a trial that the king ordered him home and appointed a replacement.

Before the former governor died, Charles said of Berkeley:

"The old fool hath put to death more people in that naked country than I did here for the murder of my father."

Bacon had left Virginia with an odd problem. He had burned down its capital. His followers had retreated a few miles up the river to a place called Middle Plantation, a community of a few houses and the church of Bruton Parish which had been established in 1674. They joined with others in a movement to build a new capital there and it seemed to be an idea whose time had come. It was on high ground where there were fewer mosquitoes and the summers were cooler. It was a more central location that was easily reached by boat from inland plantations.

But instead, the men in charge rebuilt the Jamestown State House and its church and for the next several years swatted bugs and fended off riots over the price of tobacco from the same old stand.

In 1689, the same year William and Mary became the joint sovereigns of England, Dr. James Blair was appointed Commissary of the Church in Virginia. Of all the parishes he visited, his overwhelming favorite was Bruton Parish, which he selected to be the site of a college everyone agreed the colony needed.

The colony itself cooperated by levying a tax on tobacco to pay for the college, and he went off to England where he received a charter from William and Mary, as well as badly-needed funds. He also received a royal appointment to head the institution, a position he held for the next fifty years.

It wasn't easy establishing the college, but Dr. Blair was a tenacious man. It sputtered to life at Middle Plantation in 1695 with a staff of three: the president, a writing master and an "usher." The College of William and Mary was soon housed in a magnificent building designed by no less a person than Sir Christopher Wren, who said that his plan had been "adapted to the nature of the country by the gentlemen there." In spite of the apparent tampering by a committee, the building turned out to be the most magnificent in the entire British Empire. In the years since, it has survived "improvements" by later architects as well as two major fires. Today it has been restored to its original appearance and it is still one of the great buildings in the entire world, not to mention its status as the only building in America by the great architect of Saint Paul's Cathedral in London.

Not long after construction began, the State House in Jamestown was destroyed by fire and the idea of moving it to another city was raised again. Since Middle Plantation had such a beautiful place for the Assembly to meet, the governor decided to move it there. In the legislation that made it possible, it was also decided to rename the town Williamsburg in honor of the king. Privately-owned buildings on the 300-acre site were bought and torn down to make way for a planned city that would be the envy of America and even the world.

The governor, Francis Nicholson, ordered that every building lot must be no less than a half-acre to allow room for a house, a garden and an orchard. He specified the distance from the street to the front door of every house should be at least six feet. Every lot was required to be fenced or walled within six months after the house was built. In these days of suburban zoning regulations, these rules don't seem at all unusual. But in 1699 they must have raised a lot of eyebrows in freedom-loving Virginia.

The governor specified that the city should have a broad main street a mile long between the college and the capitol. It would be 90 feet wide and named Duke of Gloucester Street. Halfway along its length would be a market square and at right angles to it would be another broad avenue leading to the governor's home, which would be called a "palace."

He had a great sense of politics, and proposed that the city should take the form of a monogram of the letters "W" and "M" to honor the king and queen. No one dared tell him that such an arrangement would have streets dropping off into ravines. Fortunately, he figured that out for himself and proposed an alternative based on a plan advanced 30 years before by Sir Christopher Wren for rebuilding the City of London after the Great Fire.

Lacking a monogram, he named the streets after the children of the monarchs. The Duke of Gloucester was the son of the queen. Another street was named for Prince George, husband of Princess Anne and Nassau Street was named for the ancestral family of the king.

Governor Nicholson was something of a tyrant, and was finally recalled. He was replaced by a man with the ironic name of Nott, who did little more for Williamsburg than leaving his name on a tombstone in Bruton churchyard. The real work of building Williamsburg and making it an important city fell on the shoulders of Alexander Spotswood, who became governor in 1710.

The job took more than ten years, during which time the streets were paved, the Governor's Palace built and Nicholson's personal coat of arms removed from the Capitol building.

Though it was among the most important cities in Colonial America, the population of Williamsburg, slaves and all, never went higher than about 2000. When the Assembly wasn't in session, it was a sleepy little country town. But when the government came to life, so did the city. The plays of William Shakespeare were presented in the evenings, featuring actors imported from London. People dressed in the height of London fashion, too. The entertaining by important people who had townhouses there was done on a lavish scale. The taverns were open all night and residents were kept awake by almost nightly fireworks displays.

But for all its importance to the history of America, Williamsburg's heyday lasted less than sixty years. When Thomas Jefferson was elected governor in 1779, British troops had already passed through Williamsburg and were threatening to come back. Jefferson proposed that the capital be moved to Richmond and when his advice was taken a year later, Williamsburg became a sleepy little college town again.

Even its history was largely forgotten by 1903 when the Rev. Dr. W.A.R. Goodwin accepted the call to become rector of Bruton Parish Church. A town native, he was dismayed by the decay that had set in even in his lifetime. He was passionate about changing it for the better and within four years he had raised enough money to restore his church to its original splendor in time for the 300th anniversary of the Episcopal Church in America. But nobody thought the whole town would ever be restored.

Dr. Goodwin moved on to Rochester, New York in 1909 and returned in 1923 to join the faculty of William and Mary. He came back with his enthusiasm intact and fortunately was able to pass some of it along to the philanthropist John D. Rockefeller, Jr. Almost no one in town didn't agree that the combination of Dr. Goodwin's passion and Mr. Rockefeller's money was the best thing that happened to Williamsburg since Governor Nicholson gave up the idea of having its streets laid out in the form of a William and Mary monogram.

On February 24, 1934, less than six years and $12 million after the restoration began, the Virginia Assembly crowded itself into the Capitol at Williamsburg for the first time in more than 150 years and officially welcomed the past back to Virginia.

The building isn't the original, but it would fool any of the original settlers. The old capitol, like so many of the Williamsburg buildings, had long since disappeared. But they have been rebuilt using original plans and, whenever possible materials from the same sources.

The Williamsburg restoration is one of the most ambitious architectural projects of the 20th century. Millions have walked its streets and taken away ideas that have changed the face of other towns all over America. It created a national interest in "recycling" rather than destroying old buildings. And all the current interest in "early American" architecture and decoration can be traced directly to this recreation of Colonial Williamsburg. The Keeper of the National Register of Historic Places has said that Williamsburg is the "formulator of popular 20th century taste" in America.

What could be more appropriate? In its relatively short life as Virginia's capital, Williamsburg was almost the formulator of America itself.

Previous page: the reconstructed Orlando Jones House of the early 18th century. Facing page and overleaf bottom right: the Margaret Hunter Shop. Top: the reconstructed house and store of John Greenhow. Above: the Public Gaol of 1701. Right: the early-18th-century Wetherburn's Tavern. Overleaf left: the Apothecary Shop. Overleaf top right: basket weaver.

Previous pages: crafts, such as cabinet-making (top left), weaving (bottom left) and cobbling (right), are kept alive in Williamsburg. Facing page: the reconstructed Raleigh Tavern, named after the man who promoted English colonization of North America in the 16th century. It was here that patriots met before issuing the call for the First Continental Congress. Far left: a cannon on Market Square and (above) the mechanism for lifting the cannon barrel onto the carriage. Left: the Union Jack atop the Capitol. Overleaf: (top left) the elegant Coke-Garrett House; (bottom left) the Deane Shop and Forge; (top right) the shops of Merchants Square and (bottom right) Chowning's Tavern.

Previous pages: John Blair
House and Kitchen on Duke of
Gloucester Street. Facing
page top: the house of
Peyton Randolph, the man who
became president of the
First Continental Congress
and whose library became
incorporated in that of
Congress. Facing page,
bottom: Orlando Jones House
and Office. Above: the
Levingston Kitchen on Palace
Green. Left: the Brush-
Everard House, which has an
unusual, U-shaped plan.
Overleaf: a colonial-style
timber yard, vital for the
construction of so many
weather-boarded houses.

Previous pages: (top left) the Raleigh Tavern; (bottom left) the rebuilt cabinetmaking workshop of Anthony Hay; (top right) the privately occupied Prentis House and (bottom right) the recreated Golden Ball, a shop of mid-18th century date. Right: the imposing facade of the Governor's Palace, which dominates Palace Green. Rebuilt on the original foundations, the present buildings are identical to those used by the British Governors in the 18th century. Below: the Capitol is a replica of that begun in 1699 and destroyed by fire in 1747, rather than that which witnessed such stirring events during the War of Independence. Facing page: the plain but elegant Bruton Parish Church of 1715. Overleaf: Duke of Gloucester Street.

Facing page: (bottom) a wagon outside the octagonal Magazine and (top) reconstructed buildings in Duke of Gloucester Street. Top left: the Sign of the Rhinoceros, a rebuilt apothecary's shop. Above: Robertson's Windmill off North England Street. Overleaf: the State Garrison Regiment and Williamsburg Militia celebrate July 4 on Market Square.

Among Williamsburg's finely reconstructed buildings are the Orlando Jones House and Office (facing page); the James Anderson House (top); the Raleigh Tavern (left) and the Printing Office (above). Overleaf: "Volley of Joy" fired by musketeers on July 4.

It is not only the buildings and bare bones of Williamsburg which are recreated; traditional crafts are also revived. Previous pages: (top left) a cobbler; (bottom left) a carpenter and (right) a chandler. Left: a craftsman at work in the Magazine which housed arms and ammunition during the French and Indian War. Top right: musicians play in the Ballroom of the Governor's Palace. Above and bottom right: traditional food and period equipment in the kitchens of the Governor's Palace. Overleaf: the Guardhouse and octagonal Magazine. The Magazine is the original, built in 1715, which played a dramatic role in the early stages of the Revolution when the governor emptied it under cover of darkness to safeguard his gunpowder.

Facing page: a musketeer holding his musket and the paper cartridge of gunpowder with which he will charge it.
Above: a collection of arms and ammunition belonging to the State Garrison Regiment. Overleaf: a parade of
troops and battle flags marks July 4 in Williamsburg.

Facing page: (top) the 17th-century John Blair House and (bottom) Chowning's Tavern. Top: the Pitt-Dixon House, in a common colonial style. Left: the Robertson's Windmill with sails set. Above: a huge chimney dominates the kitchen of John Blair House. Overleaf: the Timson House.

The costumed staff (these pages) who can be found throughout Williamsburg lend an air of authenticity to the town. Overleaf: a parade held as part of the Independence Day celebrations.

Top: the interior of Bruton Parish Church. Left: Hall of Burgessess, (above) Council Chamber and (facing page) the General Court, all within the Capitol. Overleaf: carriages in Duke of Gloucester Street and (inset) the Courthouse of 1770.

Previous pages: (top left) George Wythe House; (bottom left) Christiana Cambell's Tavern; (top right) Norton-Cole House and (bottom right) Bryan House. Right: Merchants Square, one of the first planned shopping centers in America, was built fifty years ago to match the style of Williamsburg. Below: the Prentis Store of 1740, the Pitt-Dixon House and other buildings in Duke of Gloucester Street. Facing page top: the reconstructed kitchen of John Blair House. Facing page bottom: the restored Margaret Hunter Shop, where fashionable goods were sold; the rebuilt Golden Ball, where craftsmen recreate the jewelry of James Craig, who lived here in 1765, and the reconstructed Unicorn's Horn. Overleaf: the band plays while a cannon is fired on 4 July.

Facing page: a pair of costumed carpenters use period tools to demonstrate their art. Above: wheelwrights
create their goods, which were so vital for a society based on horse transport. Overleaf: a costumed lady in
the gardens behind the richly-ornamented Governor's Palace.

Previous pages: the backs of
the reconstructed Orlando
Jones House and Office, with
their distinctive oval-plan
garden. Above: a lady
jeweler at work with period
tools. Right and top right:
the upper story and (facing
page) the dining room of
Raleigh Tavern. When news
reached Williamsburg that
the British had closed
Boston, nonimportation
measures were agreed in the
original tavern. Overleaf:
(left) basket making and
(right) spinning, two of the
crafts carried on in
Williamsburg.

Previous pages: a cannon fires a salute and (inset) musketeers fire a "Volley of Joy" on July 4. Left: Nicolson's Shop in Duke of Gloucester Street. Below: a carriage tied up in Duke of Gloucester Street, near the Norton-Cole House. Bottom left: the Prentis Store. Bottom right: the rebuilt Blue Bell, which had an unusual basement kitchen. Facing page: the roof of the Governor's Palace seen from the garden of Robert Carter House. Overleaf: Market Square.

When the Capitol (facing page) came to be rebuilt, there was a problem. Two capitols had stood on the site, one from 1699 to 1747 and the second from 1753 until 1832. It was eventually decided to rebuild the earlier structure as better information was available and a more exact replica possible. Left: the Courthouse of 1770, seen from the Guardhouse. Top left: the sign of Edinburgh Castle outside Burdett's Ordinary. Top right: the imposing gateway and facade of the Governor's Palace, built to embody British rule in Virginia. Above: Market Square. Overleaf: a baker using a period range.

Previous pages, these pages and overleaf: stirring scenes from the various military displays staged at Williamsburg throughout the year.

Previous pages and right: the original
Magazine with its rebuilt surrounding
wall. Top: Market Square Tavern, which
shows how some colonial buildings grew
by means of frequent extensions. Above:
a member of the costumed staff. Facing
page: a carriage in Market Square.
Overleaf: the Peyton Randolph House on
Nicholson Street.

Facing page: the tiny Boot and
Shoemaker's Shop in Duke of
Gloucester Street, with John Greenhow
House and Store beyond. Both have
been rebuilt in a style typical of
the period. Top: the colorful gardens,
resplendent with plants popular at
the time. Above and right: costumed
staff explaining the city. Overleaf:
the Courthouse of 1770. The
overhanging pediment seems in need of
columns, but they were not called for
in the original plan, so those added
in 1911 have since been removed.

Below: the view of the Governor's Palace from Palace Green. Right and facing page: the Palace from the formal gardens. These gardens have been recreated in the best traditions of the age. Neatly-trimmed, geometric hedges enclose equally neat flower beds, while tall trees dominate the scene and provide welcome shade from the summer sun. Elsewhere in the grounds lies a fishpond, which would have provided welcome additions to the Governor's table, and a maze. Bottom right: the Capitol. Overleaf: the house of Archibald Blair, which was erected in the mid-18th century, though the elegant porch is a later addition.

Previous pages: (left) the King's Arms Barber Shop, a rebuilt shop which houses 17th-century tools for dressing the then-fashionable wigs as well as hair, and (right) a costumed member of staff. Below: George Wythe House, a solid, brick house of the mid-18th century. George Wythe had a distinguished public career, culminating in his signing of the Declaration of Independence. Right: one of Williamsburg's smaller buildings. Bottom right: the interior of the wheelwright's workshop. Facing page: the apparently stone-faced Pasteur-Galt Apothecary Shop. Wooden boarding could be given the appearance of stone by a process known as rustification – cutting the wood to resemble stone blocks. Overleaf: Merchants Market and (inset bottom right) costumed staff.

Previous pages; costumed staff. Top: the Chamber in the Capitol, where the aristocratic Council met. Left: the reconstructed Davidson Shop, which saw service as an ordinary and an apothecary shop. Above: the tiny Boot and Shoemakers Shop and the larger Greenhow-Repiton House. Facing page: the Governor's Palace. Overleaf: costumed staff.